How to Be a World-Class Christian

The 1994 Chapel of the Air 50-Day Spiritual Adventure "Daring to Dream Again"

Never Too Late to Dream, by David Mains. Discover how to break through the barriers of your past and prejudices, your self-centeredness and anxieties, and reclaim the dreams God has planted in your heart. Book includes group discussion questions. Catalog no. 6-3203.

Back to Your Spiritual Future, by Steve Bell. As the author remembers the highs and lows of his own continuing spiritual journey, he also shares biblical principles and insights to help you refocus your priorities and get back to your spiritual future. Includes individual and group work sections. Catalog no. 6-3205.

How to Be a World-Class Christian, by Paul Borthwick. You can be a part of God's global action—from your own neighborhood to the "ends of the earth." Special 50-Day Adventure abridged edition. Catalog no. 6-3204.

Adventure Journals. Dig deeper into the adventure with day-by-day personal growth exercises. Available in the following editions:

Adult	Catalog no. 6-8830
Student	Catalog no. 6-8832
Children, grades 3–6	Catalog no. 6-8831
Critter County Activity Book	Catalog no. 6-8833

ALSO AVAILABLE

Church Starter Kit	Catalog no. 6-8838
Children's Church Leader's Guide	Catalog no. 6-8836
Small Group Starter Kit	Catalog no. 6-8839
Student Leader's Guide	Catalog no. 6-8828

How to Be a World-Class Christian

Paul Borthwick

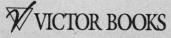

VICTOR BOOKS

A DIVISION OF SCRIPTURE PRESS PUBLICATIONS INC.
USA CANADA ENGLAND

Editor: Barbara Williams
Cover Design: Scott Rattray
Cover Photo: Image Bank

Library of Congress Cataloging-in-Publication Data

Borthwick, Paul, 1954–
   How to be a world-class Christian / by Paul Borthwick.
      p.   cm.
   Includes bibliographical references.
   ISBN 1-56476-204-1
   1. Missions. 2. Christian life—1960–   I. Title.
BV2063.B646   1993
266–dc20   93-30561
                                   CIP

Contents

Foreword

Our new 50-Day Spiritual Adventure is called "Daring to Dream Again." A lot of Christians have stopped dreaming God's dreams for them. There are reasons for this. That's why the Adventure is subtitled "Breaking through Barriers That Hold Us Back."

"Caring about our country and nothing beyond" is one of the barriers that keep the church from dreaming God's dreams. In this marvelous book, Paul Borthwick tells us how we can become a part of God's global action. He challenges us to become world-class Christians.

That phrase "world-class" doesn't mean we are to see ourselves as elite or lofty. We're not competing with Christians in other countries like a world-class athlete might compete in preparation for the Olympics. We're just attempting to bring ourselves in line with God's desires for this world.

We also want to catch up with those from other lands who even now are feeling the winds of the Spirit. You see, while we pray for revival here in North America, it's being experienced on other continents. Right now God is moving in a marvelous way throughout much of Central and South America. The same is true in Africa and Asia. Even parts of Eastern Europe are seeing unprecedented opportunities for the church to grow and touch lives inside and outside sanctuary walls.

Catching up will not be easy. The globe still seems very large to most of us. But this book does a marvelous job of taking an enormous challenge and breaking it down into tasks we can manage.

I believe we know that God is not Lord over just one nation or one people group. Those in positions of privilege, however, historically have had a hard time understanding the expansiveness of divine love. That was true of the Jews in Bible times. It's also true of North American believers in our day.

But the time to dare to dream God's dreams once again has not passed. In His graciousness, He has continued to give us ample opportunity to identify with His desires to bring all of creation under the lordship of Christ. I trust that hundreds of thousands of Adventure Team members will get a taste of what that means during this special 50-day period. If that is the case, it will not only bring joy to the Lord, but to many of us as well.

Dr. David R. Mains
Director, The Chapel of the Air Ministries

Chapter One

WHY BE A WORLD-CLASS CHRISTIAN?

*Once you decide
to ask Jesus Christ
to take control of your life,
involvement in world missions
is no longer optional.*
                    Peter Wagner

These are exciting times to be alive. Historians' veins pump with adrenaline when they observe the changes, events, developments, and growth in our world. As Marshall McLuhan predicted, our world has become a "global village." Jet travel, international networks, and interdependent economies have simultaneously shrunk the world while vastly enlarging the amount of information that we try to manage.

In the midst of this expanding base of information and the shrinking global picture, we find ourselves striving to live on a "world-class" scale. Multinational corporations attempt competition in a global market by reaching the elite distinction of becoming "world-class." Airline advertisements describe Air Canada as "World-Class, Worldwide." Television and sports networks introduce us to "world-class" athletes, and concerts highlight the performances of "world-class" musicians. The adjective "world-class" now describes automobiles, tastes of food, computer technology, hotels, lifestyles, and even disasters.

Dr. Howard Foltz, president of the Association of International Missions Services, writes, "What does it take to be world-class? Florence 'Flo-Jo' Joyner, the tough and flashy runner who won several medals at the 1988 Seoul Olympics, is a world-class athlete who breaks world records. World-class autos are those which forge a sales niche in the world market, so how would you describe a world-class Christian?"[1]

If the business, sports, and media worlds strive to compete on a "world-class" scale, what about the followers of Jesus Christ? Should we too be aiming at world-class excellence in our obedience? Are we to try to relate to the contemporary world so that the Christian faith addresses world-class problems?

The obvious answer is YES! God has given us the privilege of living at one of the most exciting, unique junctures in human history. Through a worldwide community, modern technology, and unparalleled global resources, we in the church of Jesus Christ have the opportunity to interact on a "world-class" scale as never before.

The term "world-class" as it applies to Christians does not refer to the ability to "compete" worldwide. Rather, it describes qualities of faith that are compatible, in cooperation, and in accord with what God wants to do through His people in this world.

God invites us to His world-class action. How will we respond?

But How?

We respond with a resounding, "Yes, Lord, I want to get on board!" That is, until we start to get a picture of the magnitude:

... over 5 billion people on earth;

... perhaps half of these having never heard of the love of God through Jesus;

... millions of starving, homeless, hopeless kids;

... urban sprawls of tens of millions of people.

We do not need to carry the descriptions too far. We all experience it—the phenomenon known as "compassion fatigue," the feeling of frustration which laments, "What possible difference could I make?"

The challenge of world-class living overwhelms us—until we begin to reduce the task to manageable chunks. One person likened getting a world vision to eating a 500-pound marshmallow—we know what needs to be done; we simply have no confidence that we can do it nor any idea of where to begin.

This book is about beginnings—simple steps that all of us can take to find our part in God's global action. But first, a few observations about motivation. What will keep us going as we tackle this immense task?

But Why?

With the myriad of challenges that we face in our own personal lives, we need to choose wisely how to invest our time. Is this global pursuit worthwhile? Even if we decide to start toward the world-class growth goal, what motivates us to endure?

Only a few of us will admit it, but we may be quietly asking, "What's in this for me? If I aspire toward 'world-classness,' how will I grow? Will the reward justify the effort?"

Without indulging our self-centeredness to excess, we find motivation as we observe the tangible results in the lives of those growing to be world-class Christians. Let's consider seven areas:

Stimulation. The media and entertainment world has convinced our generation that life is a spectator sport. Like Chauncy the gardener in Peter Seller's film *Being There*, "we like to watch." We watch. We watch while superior athletes compete. We experience adventure vicariously through Indiana Jones, Rambo, or Chuck Norris. Even our faith can become an experience in watching—as pastors, preachers, or dynamic personalities talk or sing or preach to us. Some have become "pew potatoes"—watching rather than participating.

Getting involved in the global scene stirs us to action. As a graduate student, I had the privilege of traveling to Haiti on an "Exposure Trip" designed to show us several international ministries there. When contemplating the trip, I confronted my first obstacle: finances—yet God miraculously made it possible for me to go. Another barrier—I had never flown before, and I (who as a child vomited when being rocked) feared my motion sickness. God took care of me—even on the twelve-seater flight to southwest Haiti, where we had to "buzz" the grass runway to clear off the grazing cows.

Every day for seven days—whether meeting Haitian Christians or speaking through a translator; whether eating unusual food or confronting a tarantula in the bathroom—I learned afresh what it meant to trust God, especially in the face of my own powerlessness. The involvement in Haiti invigorated my faith.

Very few people have ever come to me for counsel on how to quiet down their personal faith; actually, I can never remember such a request. Most of us look for ways to enliven our faith, not deaden it.

Growing as a globally aware Christian stimulates our faith to develop, as aerating soil stimulates growth in plants. It stirs us up. The pursuit of becoming world-class launches us into a world where we must trust God. Whether it means praying for the funds needed for an international project or walking out to minister in an unfamiliar neighborhood, an outward orientation of our faith encourages us to trust God in direct and practical ways.

One participant on an educational/service project to Egypt wrote: "I think the greatest lesson I learned on this trip was how to deal with difficult situations. . . . I learned this lesson because, with the nature of the trip, one had to learn these lessons to endure the experience. The work was hard, conditions uncomfortable, and amenities barely adequate—but with God's help I could withstand this and grow in my faith through the experience."

Pursuing the world-class goal puts us personally into the action. Rather than experiencing life vicariously through those we watch, *we move from being spectators to participants*. Reaching out in what might be risky relationships or volunteering for sacrificial service moves us out of our comfort zone into the arena of dependence on Christ. And, like Peter on the water, when we step out in faith, Jesus meets us there!

Focus. Don observed his own ability to be

swayed by cultural opinions and current trends. He concluded, "I am the disciple of the last man who spoke."

Don illustrates the tensions we all face regarding priorities, choices, and a clarified focus on our lives. The advertisements dictate to us what we must have to be acceptable—whether cars, clothes, vacations, or perfume. We follow the advice of a pluralistic world that dictates standards of success, but we find ourselves being torn apart. In one way or another, we fall prey to becoming cultural Christians rather than true disciples.

Tom Sine, futurist and consultant, wrote: "We all seem to be trying to live the American Dream with a little Jesus overlay. We talk about the lordship of Christ, but our career comes first. Our house in the 'burbs comes first. Upscaling our lives comes first. Then, with whatever we have left, we try to follow Jesus."[2]

We need help in focusing our lives.

In spite of the magnitude, a global awareness helps us do just that. Alertness to the needs of others, concern for the broken people of our world, and ideas of how to respond practically give us a new sense of priorities. Rather than an unhealthy preoccupation with the question, "Am I fulfilled?" we find ourselves asking how we can help others—and, in so doing, we find the fulfillment we were looking for in the first place.

A businessman in the financial district of Boston told me that serving meals at a soup kitchen for Boston's homeless clarifies the meaning of his life. "It makes me see myself as a fellow-struggler with these people, and this helps me keep my world and my problems in perspective."

Joy. Similar to that businessman, the Lands family added perspective to their lives by serving the Thanksgiving meal at a shelter for the homeless. Rather than gorging themselves on the typical — "I ate too much, where's the Alka-Seltzer?" — Thanksgiving dinner, they decided to go out to serve. Their practical yet sacrificial service produced greater thankfulness than they had known on any previous Thanksgiving.

One of the teenage daughters reflected, "At first we thought we would feel more thankful because we would realize how much more we had than these people did, but the greatest memory of the day for me is joy: These folks who seemed to have nothing could give and experience joy together. Sharing in their joyful simplicity taught us far more than we gave them."

Venturing out into our exciting, frightening, hurting world teaches us that Jesus-type joy is joy in the face of hardship, joy in spite of the surroundings. An outward focus puts us in touch with the joy that Paul the Apostle had in jail when he wrote in his most joy-filled epistle, "Rejoice in the Lord always" (Phil. 4:4). And this joy keeps us going through the roller-coaster ride of life.

Relevance. I asked a number of unchurched people their opinions about Christians: "Who would you say is the best example of Christianity the way it's supposed to be?"

A few answered "Billy Graham" because of his public integrity, but the vast majority answered "Mother Teresa of Calcutta." The reason? "Because she's the only one that I see who treats poor people the way that Jesus would."

Nobody commented much about her theology, her nun's habit, or her tiny stature. The dominant feature of Mother Teresa in the minds of these secular people was her active, demonstrated faith. Their comment reminded me of the rebuke attributed to the existentialist Nietzche: "His disciples will have to look more saved if I am to believe in their Savior."

Growing as a world-class Christian helps us "look more saved." When we explain that we spent our weekend helping people insulate their homes or serving at a nursing home, people may inquire more about the faith that motivates such action. When we spend a vacation visiting missionary friends, people ask us about our experiences, which inevitably leads to a discussion of our beliefs.

World-class involvement builds credibility because we begin to take an interest in world-class issues—whether political, religious, or environmental. My wife, Christie, strives to address the Gospel values to rain-forest destruction in South America; in so doing, she is able to integrate her faith with issues raised by environmental activists. One non-Christian man came to hear me preach because I gained credibility in his eyes by getting involved in the township of Soweto, South Africa.

An outward focus of our faith—integrated into our world and addressed to real needs and issues—establishes our witness to the mercy of Jesus as credible, demonstrable, and relevant. Our world needs to see followers of Christ who indeed love mercy and do justice (Micah 6:8).

In the ever-shrinking global village that God sends us into, the world is asking, "What type of neighbors will these Christians be?" When we dive into service and start participating in the demonstration of Jesus' love, people start paying attention.

Direction. Stephanie started growing as a world-class Christian several years ago. For her, that growth led to involvement with international students, most notably scholars from the People's Republic of China. Working together with several friends, she used her gift of hospitality to entertain, feed, and love dozens of Chinese visitors.

After a few years of this ministry, she decided to go to China for a visit. She took a leave of absence from her engineering firm and traveled five weeks in China, staying with men and women whom she had befriended on their visits to the United States. After her rugged trip, including bronchitis and a stint in a Beijing hospital, I thought Stephanie would be quitting her ministry to the Chinese or at least she would never travel again.

Quite the contrary! After her return, she made contact with the English Language Institute. She applied, was accepted and trained, and is now teaching English at a technical school in Beijing.

Outreach into the world beyond her normal sphere of influence put Stephanie in a new position to hear God. Her firsthand involvement gave new direction to her life. Not everyone gets so radically redirected. Some find new ways to use their skills to serve—like Bob, a Boston architect. He heard of an urban mission that needed help as they redesigned and refurbished their building to house residents. In his spare time, and at no cost to the mission, he used his architectural skills to design a new wing for the mission. In so doing, he saved them thousands of dollars while feeling the satisfaction of using his skills to help others.

Or consider Pat, who uses her teaching

skills to tutor urban students once a week.
Because of her time spent with students, she
has built a new network of friends, developed
a new appreciation for the city, and helped
students go from "F's" to "B's."

When we get tired of "grabbing for all the
gusto" because we find it empty or dissatisfy-
ing, God says, "I have a better way: service in
behalf of others." Jesus taught it—if you want
to be great, become a servant; if you want to
be first, then become last (Mark 10:43-45).
Jesus' paradox: We gain by losing; we lead by
serving; we find ourselves by giving ourselves
away. In the process of serving we find new
purpose and direction for the skills, abilities,
and resources that He has given us.

Sneak Previews. Any major motion picture
lures us out early to catch the sneak previews
so that (I presume) we can be the first to be
able to describe the characters and plot to our
friends.

God invites us to a sneak preview too.
Through growth as world-class Christians, we
have the unique opportunity of getting a
sneak preview of heaven, where those from
every nation, tribe, people, and language will
worship Jesus together (Rev. 7:9).

As a participant of the Lausanne II Conference in Manila, I marveled at the opening and
closing ceremonies, where representatives
from 190 countries—in national dress, some

with flags, others with instruments—led our celebration and our singing. People from many races, tribes, languages, and countries gathered together to sing praise to Jesus, the Lamb of God, who takes away the sins of the world. I thought to myself, "This is what heaven will be like!"

In a microcosm, we can get similar previews by worshiping with believers from other countries, who worship in other languages, follow other traditions, and sing in different tones. Without traveling more than twenty miles, I can worship with brothers and sisters from Brazil, China, Laos, or Haiti. As I worship with them—with all of the cultural "dressing" their service might include—I develop an enlarged vision of the body of Christ. This in turn enlarges my vision for His world and my vision of who He is—the Lord of the universe, the hope of the world.[3]

Pleasure. Put simply, our efforts to grow as world-class Christians please God. They please God because in the process we imitate Christ (Phil. 2:5-11)—serving without reciprocation. Every year, our church sends out volunteers to serve in various ways on mission teams. At least once each summer someone is asked, "Well, who pays you to do this?"

The team member explains, "No one. Actually, we pay to be able to serve on the team."

The amazed inquirer inevitably responds,

"You mean you *pay to work?*"

They pay to serve because they are following the example of Jesus, who paid (with His own life) for the opportunity to serve us — even while we were still spiritually dead in our sins! (Rom. 5:8)

Outward-focused serving pleases God because it puts us at His disposal — workers in His "harvest fields" (Matt. 9:36-38). Developing a world-class discipleship pleases God because in so doing, we break out of the entrapments of cultural Christianity and open ourselves to see Him with greater love and to serve Him with renewed vigor.

You Are Invited — Do You Accept?

I feel hurt when I find out, after the fact, that my friends had a party and I was not invited. Whether by reason of unintentional oversight or deliberate rejection, no one likes to be left out.

The good news is this: God invites us into His worldwide action! No one is left out. The magnificent, awesome task requires every Christian to participate. We cannot do it alone, but we join together so that as we grow to be world-class Christians, the world-class church will get God's work — the Great Commission[4] — done.

David Bryant, leader of a movement called "Concerts of Prayer," teaches that God's primary goal is *not* to get each of us into the

Great Commission. His goal is to get the Great Commission *into us!* God invites us into His worldwide action in order to change our lives. As we jump in, it will make us more like Jesus and help us to experience all that God has for us. Let's go for it!

Chapter Two

INFORMATION AND ISSUES

*A world-class Christian lifestyle
is compatible with what
God is doing in our world.*

Anthropologists identify the earliest stages of societies as "hunters and gatherers," those people who foraged through the fields and forests gathering berries and roots and other edibles for their sustenance. I like to think of world-class Christians as "hunters and gatherers" in a different way. To further our growth, we are always hunting for information and gathering data about issues in the world into which God calls us. We continue to grow by foraging through books, newspapers, and a host of other sources to expand our minds concerning God's great world.

Hunting for information and gathering data is a lifelong challenge, so let's consider some of the habits of world-class Christians.

Information

Do we live in a global village or not? While those who focus their lives on missions continue to discuss the miniaturization of our world, many seem to be increasingly ignorant about the world and its affairs. It is almost as if the rich are getting richer (i.e., those whose jobs are global in nature continue to learn about intercultural issues, worldwide developments, and international economies) while the poor get poorer (i.e., those who are not required to learn about world issues diminish in their knowledge of what is happening around the globe).

Brian O'Connell cited an incident several years ago when sixteen candidates for a senatorial seat were given a "pop quiz" on current events. Of five questions, only one candidate answered more than two questions correctly. O'Connell concluded: "Unfortunately, this lack of knowledge among leaders reflects a lack of information and concern for international affairs among the bulk of our society. Almost without exception, polls show that Americans are uninformed and unconcerned about international events."[1]

Is this lack of knowledge any less among Christians? Happily, I have found that an increased desire to know God's purposes in the world is leading many Christians to grow in their concern for world events. Pastors include global issues in their pastoral prayers.

Churches rise up to care for refugees in their areas. Missionaries find increased interest in global issues when they bring their reports home, and international Christian leaders find themselves issuing challenges from many North American pulpits.

But we still have many opportunities to grow!

Gathering global information can help us continue to build a world-class Christian vision. Where to start? How about purchasing an up-to-date map? A missions committee asked me what they could do to expand their church's world vision. I suggested a world map in a prominent place in the foyer. One member proudly responded, "We already have one." I went to see it.

The huge map covered the wall facing the sanctuary. Everyone would see it when they walked in. That was the good news. The bad news? The map still had countries with names like Rhodesia, The Belgian Congo, and French Indo-China on it rather than Zimbabwe, Zaire, and Vietnam. Anyone who knew the modern world would look at this map and think, "This church has a world vision, but they are considerably out of date."

One school of business management, encouraging readers to "take global education seriously," wrote:

American citizens may be among the

world's most prosperous, but according to a recent *National Geographic* study conducted by the Gallup Poll, their geographical knowledge is hardly world-class. In the nine-nation survey of 10,820 adults, U.S. respondents finished third from the bottom. . . . Among the American respondents, 75 percent failed to locate the Persian Gulf on a map. At the same time, fewer than half could find the United Kingdom, France, South Africa, or Japan. Using blank maps, the average American could identify only four of twelve European nations, and fewer than six of ten U.S. states. Perhaps most humiliating, one in seven U.S. adults could not identify the United States on a map.[2]

Buy a map! Or better yet, how about a copy of Patrick Johnstone's *Operation World*? This international handbook for Christians outlines every country of the world over the course of 365 days, gives pertinent data, and then offers specific prayer requests for the country of the day. *Operation World* (which is updated about every three years) provides an excellent source of global information while helping us with our geography. (For specifics, see the resource list in the back of this book.)

Knowing the world in which we live is essential for effective functioning as world-class Christians. Gilbert Grosvenor of the *National*

Geographic warns, "Our adult population, especially our young adults, do not understand the world at a time in our history when we face a critical economic need to understand foreign consumers, markets, customs, opportunities, and responsibilities."[3]

Grosvenor's concern is economic. Our concern goes beyond that, since God calls us to be His ambassadors (2 Cor. 5:20). Ignorance of our world can discredit our witness. An international student from Peru told me of being introduced to an American who said, "Oh yes, Peru, the islands off the coast of Ecuador."

"No," the student politely replied, "You are thinking of the Galapagos Islands. Peru is the country directly below Ecuador."

"No, I think you are incorrect," the American replied belligerently, and the conversation came to an abrupt halt.

My Peruvian friend told me that the conversation was not ruined by the American's incorrect location of Peru. Many international people are tolerant of our geographic ignorance. "It was his arrogance, telling me that I did not know where my own country is." An opportunity lost as an "ambassador for Christ" because of arrogance added to geographic ignorance.

Reading can further our informational growth. A myriad of rich opportunities are available to us through the printed media. Larry, the chairman of our missions committee, is a self-taught missions specialist. By trade he is an electrician, but a unique situation in his job grants him some time to read. His global information gathering, unsurpassed in our church, includes missions periodicals, biographies, books about mission strategy, and even sections of David Barrett's mammoth work, *The World Christian Encyclopedia.* Larry stands as an example to us all that the information is out there if we are willing to discipline ourselves to read.

For some, disciplined reading comes only as a result of being in a structured learning situation. A course on international business, cross-cultural understanding, or even geography and history might serve as a catalyst for world-class learning. The "Perspectives" Course (out of the U.S. Center for World Mission), which provides an excellent overview of the world Christian movement, can stimulate any Christian to read and thus gain a broader understanding of our world.

World-class information gathering can also include reading the international section of the newspaper, catching excerpts of God's work around the world through publications from missions agencies, or consulting global reports such as *Church Around the World*[4] or those produced by the Evangelical Missions Informations Service.[5]

Radio, television, and movies can foster greater growth in our gathering of information. One friend listens to radio station HCJB out of Quito, Ecuador "simply to hear the Gospel going out in another language." Another listens to National Public Radio because it offers more in-depth reporting on international events (which may not even be covered by network news stations).

Cable News Network opens global horizons to us. Some grow by watching programs related to cultures, nature, or international events featured on PBS. *National Geographic* specials take us around the world, educating us and giving us fuel for global praying about people, cultures, and places that we may never see firsthand.

One friend collects videos about other parts of the world. *Out of Africa, Passage to India, Gandhi,* and others have some value in educating us about culture and history, and they can provide enjoyable ways for us to learn. *Chariots of Fire* offers us information and insight about the great missionary Eric Liddell.

In all this learning, the goal is not merely cognitive growth. Instead, we seek out information so that we might be more effective "ambassadors for Christ" in the immediate world into which He sends us. One man, after hearing a radio report of testimonies from the Lausanne II Conference in Manila of the Gospel going forward in the face of hardship, wrote, "A report like that makes it easy for guys like me to go out into the marketplace during the week with motivation to present the Gospel with excitement."

What do missionaries do? Answering this question further stirs our knowledge of God at work in the world, but many of us need more contemporary answers. Past images of white, pith-helmeted missionaries carrying the Gospel to helpless savages desperately need updating. Cross-cultural workers now come from every continent and go to every continent. The Third World international ministry force will soon surpass the number of personnel from traditional "sending countries."

And not every cross-cultural worker plants churches. Some, working with relief and development ministries, plant plants. "Tentmakers" use business, teaching, medical, and engineering skills to gain access to countries that do not allow traditional missionaries. Some international "ambassadors of Christ" go as pioneers to primitive tribes working in inaccessible jungles, but many others go now as pioneers in modern cities working in urban jungles.

World-class information gathering means enlarging our vision of what is being done (and what remains to be done) by the international network of Christian workers in a variety of contexts and cultures.

One last word about information gathering: Make it fun! Learning about cultures might include an international meal. Studying the map does not require sitting in the library; instead, buy a world map beach ball and read it while getting a tan. My friend Larry does an enormous amount of reading, but this includes children's books—from picture books to coloring books to easy-to-read biographies like *My Book about Hudson* (about Hudson Taylor).

Expand your world knowledge and have some geographic fun by trying to decipher twelve capitals of Europe from these:[6]

1. LOBS IN
2. DID ARM
3. SHIN-LIKE
4. I SPAR
5. A TRAIN
6. GEAR UP
7. LEG BEARD
8. WAS RAW
9. CUB'S HEART
10. OPEN CHANGE
11. HAS TEN
12. NON-OLD

Issues

Hunting for international information coincides with gathering data pertaining to issues that threaten the spread of the Gospel. While there are hundreds of issues that any of us could focus upon, there are several "mega-issues" that we all should at least be aware of (and perhaps which every church should give at least partial consideration to during the course of the year).

Morris Watkins identifies some of these "mega-issues" in *Seven Worlds to Win*. He points out the greatest challenges facing the spread of worldwide Christianity as:

1. The Chinese world (one of every five people on earth)
2. The Hindu world (and the "New Age" carryover into the Western world)
3. The Buddhist world (much of South Asia)
4. The Muslim world (with a zeal to do its own brand of "evangelizing")
5. The Communist world (which is ever changing)
6. The Bibleless/illiterate world (over 3,000 languages yet to receive their own translation of the Bible and some countries with 95 percent illiteracy)
7. The So-Called Christian world (where Christianity is traditional but not personal)[7]

Floyd McClung and Kalafi Moala, in *Nine Worlds to Win*, include Watkins' "mega-issues" numbers 2, 3, 4, 5, and 7 and expand it further to include:

1. The world of the Poor and Needy (1 billion hungry people; thousands of slum neighborhoods around the world; 1 million street people in Calcutta)
2. The Urban world (with an estimated 75 percent of the world living in urban centers by the year 2010 and currently

over 300 world-class cities (with populations exceeding 1 million)
3. The world of Youth and Children (over 35 percent of the Third World under age 15 and 50 percent under 25)
4. The Tribal world (many of the 12,000 "hidden peoples" with no access to the Gospel)[8]

Any list like this oversimplifies our world, but it provides a helpful tool to assist us in getting a grasp of the major issues facing the church around the world. Any one of these issues—or others that we may want to pursue, such as the staggering growth of the Third World missionary movement (people being sent from the non-Western world across cultures), or the AD 2000 Movement (cooperative efforts to complete the task of world evangelization by the year 2000), or the remaining unreached peoples (12,000 distinct cultural groupings with no witnessing church in their midst)—can occupy us for the next decade, but a little information about each issue and specific information on one issue can help us to be acutely aware of the challenges ahead.

Implementation
Hunting for information and gathering data on issues—how can it be done? Any reasonable person could discount the above suggestions

as unreasonable in light of the vast amount of information available.

But instead of getting overwhelmed, why not get started? Choose an issue, a country, a "people-group," and dive in:

1. Pray for God to start giving you opportunity to learn about your study topic. Several of our students started praying two years ago about Burkina Faso, West Africa. Suddenly they started noticing articles, seeing TV programs, and meeting people related to that tiny country. As they prayed, God opened new horizons of opportunity to learn.

2. Start clipping articles from the newspaper or news magazines and create your own files. I never realized how much was being written on Mozambique until several years ago when, in preparation for a trip there, I started a file. Now it bulges with articles that help me understand and pray for the church in that country.

3. Go to the library and look up recent books (or, in *The Reader's Guide to Periodical Literature*, recent articles) on your topic. With so many events changing our world, a trip to the library every one or two months is necessary, especially if your study topic is a "hotspot" that is often in the news.

4. Use cross-cultural friends. When Nelson Mandela was released from jail in South Africa, I called some friends who live in Soweto (a township outside of Johannesburg) for a re-

port. A phone call (costing about $10) gave me a firsthand report that was greater and more personal than any news broadcast.

5. Attend a seminar or lecture on your topic. Bill, a friend interested in China and especially Tibet, recently went to a lecture at a nearby college given by two scholars from Lhasa, Tibet's capital. Cultural lectures at museums, libraries, or colleges are often free of charge and provide excellent opportunities for questions.

6. Pool your information. A group studying massive issues like AIDS in Africa or hunger in Asia will accumulate much more information than any one individual—and group learning can be stimulating and fun.

Look What God Is Doing
The leaders of ACMC (Advancing Churches in Missions Commitment) encourage world-class Christians to develop a bifocal vision:

- *nearsighted:* looking close at hand to the needs right around us, and
- *farsighted:* looking beyond ourselves to the world of need and opportunity outside our normal sphere of influence.

Hunting for information and gathering data about global issues can add perspective to the world into which He calls us and power to our international prayers.

Chapter Three

OUR PRAYERS CAN BE WORLD-CLASS

Satan laughs at our toiling,
mocks our wisdom,
but trembles when we pray.
The Kneeling Christian

My wife and I sat with missionaries in Mozambique, the civil-war-ravaged country in southeast Africa. We listened to their accounts of difficulties with distributing food and clothing to people in desperate need. They sadly described the agony of thousands of people living on the edge of survival.

As they talked, a wave of helplessness overcame us. What could we possibly do? I asked the relief workers, "After we return home, is there anything we can do for you?"

They responded immediately: "Tell the people back home that we are depending on their prayers! We need God's supernatural help to continue this work."

Their answer reminded me of Paul's words

to the Corinthians in the face of great persecution and hardship. He wrote of his hope in God's provision, but noted their human responsibility by stating, "On Him [God] we have set our hope that He will continue to deliver us, *as you help us by your prayers*" (2 Cor. 1:10-11, emphasis mine).

We can join God's worldwide team—helping others by our prayers—in the endeavor of communicating the Gospel of Jesus Christ through word and deed.

We all have the incredible opportunity of participating in God's work worldwide, so why don't we? Let's consider three of the largest prayer obstacles and some ideas on how to respond to them:

Obstacle #1: *"It's too overwhelming."*
Response #1: *Pray manageably.*
All of us can be overtaken by a similar wave of helplessness—like the one that we felt in Mozambique—but we cannot succumb to the temptation to quit. The answer lies in manageable praying. I cannot pray for millions of hurting children in our world; I have difficulty focusing on Kenya, a country where 60 percent of the population is under age fourteen. But I can pray consistently for Oyie Kimasisa, the young Kenyan boy we support with World Vision. Using updates and reminders I receive from their Kenya office, I can participate in a ministry to Oyie through prayer. By concen-

trating on one child, I can manage my response in prayer.

When I asked a missionary the greatest way we (in a sending church) can encourage him, he responded immediately, "If one person in the church approached me and said, 'I have been praying for you every day,' I think I would start walking on air!" This missionary asked only that one person make it his or her manageable task to pray for him.

We can likewise pray manageably about world events. When the news reports a devastating earthquake, typhoon, or other natural disaster, manageable praying means lofting a "prayer arrow" (see pp. 44–45) – a brief prayer that we can breathe to God about the crisis. We might pray for government leaders, relief coordinators, or local church leaders – that God will guide their efforts in responding. Through a brief and manageable prayer, we can be involved in that event.

Obstacle #2: *"But what do I pray about?"*
Response #2: *Pray practically.*
We err when we think that prayer is limited to eloquent oratory in King James English. We worship the Lord who taught us to pray for our daily bread. He welcomes our practical requests.

When we pray around the world, we often lack for specifics, so we need to use our imaginations. I have started developing "ever-widening circle" praying. I start with that which I know and then move outward, letting God direct my prayers.

I might start by praying for David and Stephanie Robinson, who direct a relief and development project in a north African country. I know them and their family, so I begin by praying for needs I am aware of. Then I move outward. I might pray (as God guides my imagination):

● that they will have success that day in meetings with government officials;

● that food distribution projects will not be blocked physically by sandstorms or administratively by red tape;

● or that well-drilling projects in that country will be successful on the first attempt.

Praying in these ever-widening circles can lead us to pray by God's direction for needs that we otherwise might never know about.

Obstacle #3: *"But will it make any difference?"*
Response #3: *Pray strategically.*
Our prayers do make a difference; God promises to work through them, and many people—like our friends in Mozambique—depend on the prayers of others.

To insure the maximum effectiveness in our prayers, we pray strategically. As the Bible commands, we pray first for "kings and all those in authority" (1 Tim. 2:2), because these leaders hold the keys to the work of the Gospel going forth. We might pray for government leaders to accelerate the efforts of a development project. Or we could ask God to work even through communist leaders so that they will open the way for organizations like the English Language Institute to bring the Gospel through teachers in countries like Mongolia.

Strategic praying also calls us to pray for Christian leaders who guide the efforts of Christian work in their nations—like Dr. Theodore Williams in South India, Claude Noel in Haiti, Ajith Fernando in Sri Lanka, or Beatrice Zapata in Guatemala. (If you would like to pray for specific Christian leaders around the world, write to World Evangelical Fellowship, P.O. Box WEF, Wheaton, IL 60189 for suggestions.)

Join God's Worldwide Team—Pray!

Paul wrote about Epaphras in his letter to the Colossians. Epaphras distinguished himself because he was "always wrestling in prayer" for those Colossian believers (Col. 4:12).

We can be like Epaphras, wrestling in prayer for people we may never meet or to which we cannot personally respond. Through prayer we have the privilege and opportunity to touch our world.

David Howard, former general director of the World Evangelical Fellowship, shared some world-class praying in his book, *The Great Commission for Today.*

Howard was a missionary in Colombia, South America, where God seemed to be answering many prayers. There were new believers everywhere, and God was mightily at work.

At the same time, Dave's older brother Phil toiled among the Slavey Indians in Canada's Northwest Territories. Phil had worked with these Indians fourteen years without one convert.

In a prayer meeting with the Indians of his village, Dave shared his concern for his brother Phil. The village leader rose and invited the people to pray. Dave described what happened: "He didn't have to repeat the invitation. Two hundred people went to their knees immediately and began to pray. Their custom is for all to pray out loud together.... That evening they prayed for one hour and fifteen minutes without stopping. They poured out their hearts for Phil, his wife, Margaret, and for those Slavey Indians."[1]

The Colombian Indians' concern for Phil continued long after that prayer session. They sent letters to encourage him and persevered in prayer. David Howard found out later that Phil, after fourteen years of seemingly fruitless ministry, had reached an all-time low. He thought, "What's the use?" and wondered why he should continue. One night he went to bed defeated and discouraged; the next day he awoke with a new joy and courage to continue the work to which God had called him.

When the brothers compared dates, the times coincided exactly: The very night that Phil went to bed ready to quit and awoke revived was the night that those Colombian Indians had spent time in zealous prayer on his behalf.

We can wrestle in prayer as part of our partnership in the worldwide body of Christ. Whether we pray regularly for the ongoing work of a development project in Bangladesh, or for one child in Kenya, or loft a prayer arrow for evangelistic efforts in Armenia, we are essential parts of God's team.

Building Our Global Praying: 10 Steps to Get Started

Step 1: Start Where We Are and Build.[2] If we have never prayed for a missionary, the church in other countries, or leaders in foreign governments, let's get started! But don't be overwhelmed at the beginning by adding 168 countries or thirty-five missionaries all at once. If we are praying for no one in another land now, we can start by adding one person. When this becomes established in our discipline of praying, we can add others.

At our church, we publish a prayer calendar to help keep the international ministry family before the congregation. After the first edition, a zealous supporter of prayer and missions asked, "Why do you have only two pictures per month?" (He had hoped that we would have at least ten to twelve each month.) I explained, "If we had so many pictures that casual observers felt overwhelmed, what good would that do? We are trying to reach people who are just getting started, and two people are easier to pray for than ten."

We can all start small. There are 46,000 or more North American missionaries. Experts talk of over three times that number from Third World sending countries by the year 2000. I cannot fathom those numbers. But I can handle one or two.

Step 2: Practice Prayer Arrows. The biblical mandate to "pray without ceasing" (1 Thes. 5:17, NASB) requires us to try to live in an attitude of prayer. This attitude can include the lofting of prayer arrows—short prayers offered on the run or in response to an immediate need. Very few of us can pray for all of the countries of the world, but we can launch a prayer arrow for a country that we hear about in the news, an international worker that pops into our minds while we are driving, or a national church that is facing unusual challenges.

I use any means available to help me pray around the world. The other day, I put on a shirt and noticed that the label read, "Assembled in Mauritius." I stopped to offer an arrow prayer for the church in Mauritius, those that work there as missionaries, and the spiritual challenges they face. Then I realized how little I knew about Mauritius, so the next day, I got my copy of *Operation World* and learned about more specific ways to pray for that island nation.

Other catalysts for arrow prayers might include the labels on bananas (which often identify the country where the bananas were harvested), names of companies that provoke world-class thoughts (like "Global Van Lines"), or reading the "Arrivals/Departures" screen while waiting to pick someone up at the airport.

Step 3: Fuel Prayer with Information. The generic "bless the missionaries" or "guide the church around the world" prayers are far too expansive. We need information about specific people and places to help our prayers. The resources like Operation Mobilization Prayer Cards (see resources) or *The Church Around the World* (see notes for chap. 2) provide helpful facts to get us started.

A missionary family in Kenya told me that they were chagrined to return home on one furlough and hear that people had been praying for their protection from leopards. The missionary responded, "We have been in Kenya eighteen years, and we have prayed to see a leopard without success. In all our years in East Africa, we have never heard of one missionary being attacked by a leopard. Instead, dozens of our friends have been injured or killed in car accidents. We need people to pray about the real dangers we face—like the highways!"

Prayer letters, international missions periodicals, or direct contact with those working overseas can provide the fuel we need for intelligent, accurate praying. When we pray for our friends in Quito, Ecuador, our first inclination is to think, "They live on the equator in South America; therefore, I will pray for God to give them grace to withstand the high heat and tropical humidity." A little information changes our prayer; after we find out that Quito (at 9,000 feet) has year-round daytime temperatures of 70 degrees and nighttime temperatures of 55, we pray, "God, help us not to be jealous of our friends' weather in Quito!"

Step 4: Pray as Part of Our Correspondence. The New Testament Epistles include some excellent prayers on behalf of churches or individuals. Paul prayed for these churches as he wrote. We can do the same as we develop our ministry of correspondence and encouragement with missionaries and friends from other countries. As we write to them, we can let the Holy Spirit teach us how to pray for them.

Bob Hill, a teacher at Greater Europe Mission's Greek Bible Institute in Athens, suggests combining prayer and correspondence: "Keep track of missionaries' current prayer needs and find out what requests have been answered. If you have been praying about something daily for several months, write to ask how the Lord is working with regard to the subject. Ask about special needs. Some items cannot be shared with the general public, and your missionary will appreciate your praying for these needs as well."[3]

Step 5: Participate in the Team Effort of Prayer. While individual intercession is a necessary discipline, group prayer is a powerful tool of God to guide the participants in "agreeing together" (Matt. 18:19). Groups like Concerts of Prayer, the Frontier Fellowship of the U.S. Center for World Missions (see resources), or other mission-agency sponsored groups can encourage global intercession.

I am ashamed of the number of times I have told people I would pray for them and then forgotten. Corporate prayer helps me grow in faithfulness. Joining together with other brothers and sisters in Christ helps me face the magnitude of the task because I share the intercession with them.

Dr. Stanley Allaby, pastor of the Black Rock Congregational Church in Connecticut, told a seminar of church mission leaders how he became convinced of the need for faithful, corporate prayer for the missions family. "Early in my ministry," he said, "we sent out our church's first 'home-grown' missionaries. This family was the pride of our missions department.

"After their first term was over, they returned to our church for a year. At the close of the year, I asked the husband, 'So, Phil, when will you be heading back overseas?'

"Phil responded, 'Pastor, I'm not sure we're going back.'

" 'Why not?' I responded.

" 'Well, Pastor, after a year here at the church, I am just not convinced that the church has been and will be praying for us.' "

Allaby went on to describe his own personal repentance and his commitment to lead the church in corporate prayer on behalf of the international family that they had sent out. "Through the honesty of that missionary," Allaby concluded, "I became convinced that we must be true to our commitments because our missionary family is depending on us."

Step 6: Find a Personal Plan. When I am inspired to build the discipline of prayer in my own life, I am tempted to copy the person who has motivated me. If sixteenth-century reformer Martin Luther rose at 4 A.M. to pray, then I want to do the same. Imitation is a great learning tool, but we must develop our own patterns for effective prayer. Some will pray well as they jog; others need complete silence. A few will like the idea of all-night vigils once per month. Others do better with fifteen consistent minutes every day. We need to find a plan that works for our lifestyle, metabolism, and spiritual maturity.

One student told me that his prayers for the world Christian movement became consistent when he put a map of the world on the ceiling over his bed. "When I first awake, the map reminds me to pray for the world—starting with the world into which I am sent, but extending beyond my friends to people I pray for in other countries."

The folks at the Caleb Project advocate a prayer plan that moves from the broadest topics to the most specific. In praying for Muslims in New Delhi, India, they start with prayer at the *macro level* (Muslims worldwide). Then they progress inward, praying at the *country level* (India), at the *city level* (New Delhi), the *people level* (Muslims as opposed to Hindus), the *church level* (for the evangelistic efforts of the Indian church), at the *laborer level* (for specific Indian Christians who are trying to reach these Muslims), and finally at the *personal level* (how does God want me to respond personally?).[4]

Step 7: Choose Appropriate Tools. Prayer should never be mechanical, but there are tools that can increase our effectiveness in prayer. The tools that we choose might be prayer cards of specific missionaries, maps, or prayer guides like the Frontier Fellowship guide. We may also want to think of our prayer posture as a tool. Some of us will choose to intercede in a kneeling posture beside a bed or chair. Others will choose to stand or sit.

During a recent bout with sleeplessness, I tried a new tool—praying through the alphabet around the world. One night I focused on cross-cultural workers I knew whose last names began with A through Z. I got stuck on X (so I prayed for missionaries who followed the example of Francis Xavier by going to serve in East Asia), but in general, it was a productive prayertime, much more useful than counting sheep.

Another night I decided to pray for countries: Algeria, Belgium, Chad, Dominica, Egypt, etc. The stumpers? Q is limited to Qatar (although I added a prayer for Quito, Ecuador). Z seemed tough, until I remembered places in Africa—Zambia, Zimbabwe, Zaire, and even Zanzibar and Zululand. The toughest again was X; I could not come up with anything, so in the morning I looked in a missions dictionary. In the future, I will remember the Xhosa people of South Africa when I pray around the geographical alphabet.

Step 8: Remember to Intercede. The Pauline

prayers from his letters to the Colossians or Philippians should guide our intercession. Effective global intercession will mean prayer for spiritual growth, victory in spiritual warfare, and effectiveness in the face of opposition for brothers and sisters around the world. If our petitions are superficial or preoccupied with physical needs, we may never experience the power of answered prayer.

Carl, a missionary in South America for twenty years, lamented after a furlough visit home, "In multiple visits with all of my supporting churches, no one has asked me about my spiritual health, and when I came home last June, my spiritual life was in a state of disrepair. I wasn't praying, my Scripture reading had lapsed, and I was thinking of quitting the ministry. People should never think that because I am a missionary, I am automatically spiritual."

Carl makes a valid point. People who serve in "professional" ministry need prayer for faithfulness in Bible reading, diligence in witnessing, and perseverance in praying. In other words, interceding effectively means praying for them about the same spiritual struggles that we encounter on a daily basis.

Step 9: Pray by Faith (Not by Results). The church in China, the Gospel's advance in Muslim countries, and the growth of Christians in little-known areas such as Albania,

North Korea, or Mongolia compel us to pray by faith. We commit these places and believers to the Lord—believing that He is at work, even when we do not see it!

In 1983, my wife and I took our first trip to East Africa. We experienced some of the results of the great East African revival as we met many men and women who were training for church leadership. In spite of the breakthroughs, however, we sensed a burden to pray for the Maasai people who—at that point—had still been quite resistant to the Gospel. Without much information, but with hope, we continued.

In 1988, we began to hear of some breakthroughs, and in 1989, I had the privilege of meeting Mary, a Maasai Christian who served as a schoolteacher. She shared the movement of the Holy Spirit in bringing many Maasai to Jesus Christ.

For Christie and me, it was a lesson in faith—praying for five years concerning people we scarcely knew. But God demonstrated His faithfulness in response to our prayers and the prayers of thousands of others for the Maasai. We remembered to pray at the urge of God's Spirit and not by tangible results.

Step 10: Learn to Say No. If we are to be effective in our intercession, we must learn to live within our own limitations of time and concentration ability. As we pray globally, we will find ourselves besieged with requests to pray more. If we are to be faithful in the priorities that we sense from God, we will need to say no. Most of us cannot pray for thousands of people by name or even hundreds of geographic areas. We need to learn to say no so that we continue to be faithful intercessors in a few areas. In general, faithfulness in prayer leads to fruitfulness in ministry; failure in prayer (committing ourselves to pray for too many people or needs) leads to frustration.

A man called me and asked for a meeting. He wanted to explain his ministry to me in hopes that our church could support him financially. I told him that we had no finances available. He responded, "Well, brother, could I come meet with you so that you could be on my prayer team?" Earlier in my life, I would have said yes simply out of guilt. But I was just learning this principle of saying no to unrealistic demands. I responded, "Brother, I must tell you the truth. If you came to meet with me, I would pray for you here in my office, but probably not again. I have joined the prayer team of many international workers, and I know I am not faithful in praying for them, so I must say no to your invitation to be on your team." He was miffed at my honesty, but I determined that I must say no rather than lie by pretending I would pray for him as he had asked.

A Worldwide Ministry

Friends in Mozambique asked us to tell the people in our church that they depended on their prayers. The Apostle Paul faced turmoil and opposition with confidence because he counted on the Corinthian believers to help him by their prayers.

We face the awesome challenge of helping others in their mission work around the world by supporting them through our prayers. Somewhere in the world, fellow Christians depend on our prayer partnership. Let's do our part to get the job done.[5]

Chapter Four

REACHING THE WORLD THAT HAS COME TO US

*The alien living with you
must be treated as one
of your native-born.
Love him as yourself.*
Leviticus 19:34

The visit to the hospital in October commenced an ordeal that would last for eight months. My mother-in-law was admitted that night and began a series of surgeries, recuperations, setbacks, and rebounds which would continue to May.

For the family, the next months were times of waiting, praying, and hanging around the hospital. When the most difficult times were over, we were still going to the hospital regularly, spending almost every free evening visiting with her.

During these months, I started to ask myself, "Here I am locked into a schedule that brings me to the hospital all the time. How can I build a world-class vision here?"

The idea came to me as I overheard two hospital workers from Haiti speaking to each other in Creole: Why not initiate more conversations with other patients and hospital employees, especially those with foreign accents?

Over the next few months, I met many men and women from Haiti, several workers from El Salvador, one from Nicaragua, another from Israel. There was an emergency room doctor from Saudi Arabia, an anesthesiologist from Bombay, a medical school student from Gabon, and a nurse from Mozambique. We met others from England, Portugal, Colombia, Germany, and Japan. Even in the hallways of one Boston hospital, we grew in our understanding of the global village in which we live.

The experiences in that hospital reminded us that world-class Christian involvement does not start overseas. It starts by looking for and reaching out to the world that God has brought to us.

The Melting Pot Reality

What country has the second largest black population in the world? How about the fourth largest Spanish-speaking culture in the world? What country has the second largest Polish city, the largest Jewish population, the second largest Puerto Rican city, the second largest Hispanic population center, and some of the largest Haitian, Cuban, Dominican, and

Guatemalan cities in the world?

According to Jerry Appleby, in *Missions Have Come to America*, the answer to all of these questions is the United States.[1] Only Nigeria has a larger black population. The United States in the 1990s may overtake Argentina and become the third largest Spanish-speaking country. Chicago's Polish population is second only to Warsaw, and there are more Jews in New York City than in Tel Aviv. With over 1 million newcomers each year, the United States will have less than 30 percent of its population registered as "white Americans" in the 1990s.

The newest members of the melting pot come to us in three basic forms. *International students* from all over the world pass through U.S. Customs each year to pursue undergraduate and graduate degrees. Many come from countries that do not allow traditional missionaries, and they come with stereotypes of the United States as a "Christian" country. Appleby describes international students this way:

Temporarily uprooted from familiar social, economic, cultural, and religious surroundings, tens of thousands of international students are transplanted each year onto the soil of colleges and universities in the United States. The frontiers of foreign missions are no longer only in

Tibet, Saudi Arabia, Mongolia, and China. They are also in Boston, New York, Chicago, and Los Angeles, for they have come to the United States in the presence of international visitors.[2]

Sadly, only a fraction of these international students get to visit an American home during their studies. As a result, they return to their countries either desperately lonely and bitter about their isolation while in America or disillusioned by the thought that dormitory life exemplified the lifestyle of "Christian" America. The leaders of International Students, Inc. (ISI) estimate that as many as 70 percent of international students never get off campus into an American home. For this reason, the dream of Gordon Loux, president of ISI, is that "every international student will have one Christian friend."

The second large group of newcomers come as *immigrants*. Education, world travel, and international business have led many internationals to make the United States their home. In Boston, for example, there are over 50,000 Haitians, which is still less than half the size of "Little Haiti" in Miami (which is much smaller than "Little Havana").

In our little town of Lexington, I get my donuts from men and women from the Azores and Brazil. Large numbers of Indian and Chinese families move in regularly. After the end of the adult swim at the town pool, I was getting dressed as the children entered for their afternoon swim. Four boys came in together: one Caucasian, one black, one Indian, and one Asian. In these four friends, I could see the international scope of the youth of our town.

And city life is even more diverse. The Southern Baptists have planted ethnic churches around Boston to reach out to Haitians, Hispanics, Cambodians, Laotians, Greeks, and Arabic-speaking people. A friend of mine pastors a church in New York City where fifteen different languages are spoken. Ray Bakke, urban specialist for the Lausanne Committee for World Evangelization, says that there are ninety languages spoken in his home city of Chicago.

Like international students, many of these immigrants come from countries where they have never heard the Gospel, and yet, when they come to the United States, they find themselves isolated and alone.

The third cluster of newcomers are the *refugees*. Some estimate this population as high as 1 million. These are the political or economic exiles who have come from the Middle East, Central America, and Southeast Asia — or anyplace where turmoil might drive them out.

Refugees represent a special call to the church of Jesus Christ because they are truly the "aliens and strangers" of our world. Homeless, displaced, and alone, these people will respond with unique openness to the love of Jesus demonstrated through His people.

Refugees often bring people into our midst who might otherwise never hear the Gospel. In the northwestern United States, a group of Laotian refugees come from a mountain tribe which is classified as a "hidden people group," and yet they have been displaced to a community where the Gospel is freely preached. Christians in that area can reach people who have eluded missions outreach for decades in their own country.

Reaching Internationals—Practical Ideas

Bill and Judy have become missionaries all over the Peoples Republic of China simply by opening their home to international business people who come to the area for six months of training. Nel has a friendship evangelism ministry that affects Saudi Arabia, one of the most Muslim countries in the world. Steve is reaching many from East Asia because he is willing to spend three hours every Saturday morning tutoring immigrants who desire to learn English. Chris helped a Christian graduate student from East Africa understand and respond to the secularistic viewpoints of his professors by inviting him to join a Bible study.

The ideas are unlimited for people with some creativity. Kathy Lay and her husband used unemployment as an outreach opportunity to internationals: "When my husband was laid off from work three years ago, he frequented a small donut shop near the unemployment office. Once a week for four months he talked with the Korean owner. Three years later we are still friends with him. We were the only Americans invited to his wedding, we prayed with him as his wife delivered their son, and we have spent time with them socially and in Bible study."[3]

We do not need an enormous amount of creative genius; we only need to look around us, open our lives and our homes, and try to be friends.

Underlying all forms of outreach to internationals are at least three basic principles.

First, start on a *foundation of prayer*. Bill and Judy pray for the chance to meet people from the Peoples Republic of China in their community. Then they go and hang out at the Chinese vegetable section of their supermarket. One group of five seemed especially prepared by God. When Bill and Judy befriended them, they said, "We have two questions: First, can you help us use the public transportation? And second, we would like to go to a church; could you take us to church?"

Tom and Carolyn build on a similar foundation of prayer, and they open their house to international tenants. God has brought them Buddhist students from Malaysia, communist students from China, and Muslim students from Egypt. In each case, the students God has brought them have been very open to discussion about Jesus, and one became a Christian and is returning to his family and country with a desire to evangelize.

Don and Meg prayed for their Pakistani Muslim friend for years. She was warm to their friendship, but resistant to the Gospel, so they prayed. After six years of friendship, prayer, and occasional discussions about the person of Jesus, their friend put her faith in Christ.

Second, build on *friendship*. Friendship is the single most important ingredient in reaching out to internationals. They need friends who will help them grow comfortable with the confusing culture of the United States. One friend spent a morning orienting a family of refugees on how to use an American home—from electric stoves to flush toilets which were unlike anything they had ever seen before.

Reaching out to internationals does not require an unusual gift of evangelism; it demands only a willingness to be a friend. Many internationals come from family-oriented cultures, and they need us to invite them into our families. When Norm and Debbie invited his coworker from India over for pizza, they met his entire family. In the course of conversation, Norm and Debbie discovered that this man and his family had been in the United States for five years, and theirs was the first American home they had visited. Until that friendship started, the Indian family had depended on television to teach them about American family life!

Gordon Loux writes, "International students in the United States are particularly vulnerable to loneliness and the disruption of a new culture. They need friends who can help them adjust to American life, answer practical questions, and ease the loneliness of separation from friends and family."[4]

Here are some practical suggestions on befriending internationals:

- Meet arriving students at the airport and make sure they have housing for the first few nights. The foreign student office on college campuses will work with you on this.
- Help them find permanent housing and get settled. Show them how to read classified ads.
- Take them on orientation visits to local stores and show them how to shop.
- Orient them to the laws and street signs. Provide them with city maps and bus schedules.
- Invite them home for meals or include them in other social activities.
- Sponsor or attend activities specifically for internationals. Churches some-

times try picnics, retreats, sporting events, sightseeing tours, or trips to museums or zoos.

● Encourage those interested in learning about Christianity to attend church services or a church social event. Use the holidays of Thanksgiving, Christmas, and Easter to explain the Christian faith.

● Hold a one-day conference at the church on Christian faith, using seminars on the Bible or Christian living—integrated with lots of hospitality—to introduce internationals to the basics of faith.[5]

Finally, *be a learner*. Learning about the country from which our international friends have come, or greeting them in their native language expresses a deep interest in the people we are trying to befriend. If we want them to listen to us talk about Christianity, we reciprocate by listening to their views without condemnation or ridicule.

Joking about sacred cows with Hindus, laughing at fanatical Muslims, or demeaning the intensity of Roman Catholicism in Latin America or the Philippines is no way to show respect to our international friends. As people who believe in the value of every person, our lives should reflect respect for and a desire to understand our foreign friends.

Here again is another reason to be gathering information about our world. One international student from Cape Verde became my friend instantly simply because I knew where he lived and that he spoke Portuguese. A taxi driver in Atlanta almost drove off the road with excitement because I knew the names of three cities in his country of Nigeria. If internationals sense that we have a genuine interest in learning about their homes, they are usually very willing to share.

One final thought about learning: Some Americans grow impatient with internationals because they cannot understand the accents or the broken English. Learning implies patience. Ask international friends to speak slowly and do the same for them. (Remember to speak slower, not louder; internationals are not deaf, they are simply learning English.) The more internationals we befriend, the better we become at deciphering accents, pronunciations, and sentence structure.

The Impact

If we want to have an intense global impact in a relatively short period of time, investing in ministry to internationals is the best option. Ministering to international students usually means touching the lives of the future leaders of business, government, and education. Every time the King of Nepal or the Prime Minister of Pakistan is in the news, I lament that no one at our church took the time to try to befriend them when they were students here in the Boston area. If someone had invested two or three hours a month in reaching out to them, the course of entire nations could have been changed.

Mark Rentz, a professor at Arizona State University, writes about this impact on national leaders through international student ministry:

Last year after we invited my foreign students to dinner, my wife and I were astonished to learn that we were in all likelihood breaking bread with future leaders. One of my students, Khaled, in replying to another student's question, mentioned that his father had been president for five years.

"Of what company?" I asked.

"Of my country," he replied.

His wife nodded, adding, "President Abdullah al-Sallal, Khaled's father, is commonly referred to as having given birth to North Yemen."[6]

A couple who now teach in Oman, a devoutly Muslim nation on the Saudi Arabian peninsula, told me that the Sultan of Oman is very favorable toward Christians in his country. He contributed land for the building of churches to accommodate foreign workers. The Sultan's unusual benevolence toward Christians stems from his experiences as a foreign student in England. When he studied there, a

British Christian took him into his home and befriended him. That anonymous man's outreach now affects an entire Muslim nation.

Another result of outreach to internationals is evangelism with those who are not reachable through conventional missions. Christie, my wife, has an ongoing ministry to a lab technologist from India. She befriended him as she trained him in parasitology, and in the process, she touched a devout Hindu who had only misconceptions about Christianity up to this point.

A friend works with Chinese scholars who come to study at the Massachusetts Institute of Technology (MIT). One of the men who has come this year is from the Weega ethnic minority, one of the official "hidden people groups" listed by the U.S. Center for World Mission. If this man learns of Jesus this year, he may be God's agent for bringing the Gospel to an ethnic group which presently has no knowledge of Jesus Christ.

A businessman had a deep conviction about reaching Muslims for Christ, so he came to me about a job opportunity in Saudi Arabia. He hoped that such an assignment could put him as an evangelist near Islam's holiest city, Mecca. Further research, however, revealed that his job assignment would put him on an American compound with very little opportunity to meet Saudis. As he prayed about the opportunity, God led him to get involved in international student ministry in Boston, where there were many from Saudi Arabia whom he could befriend and evangelize freely.

A third impact of ministry with internationals relates to the training of cross-cultural workers who will go from the United States to other countries. The couple who now teach in Oman prepared by getting involved with Arabic speaking people here in Boston before they went. Now they are on their way, but as a result of ministry here in Boston, they speak Arabic fluently, and they have Arabic-speaking Christians in Boston praying for them in Oman.

When Tom and Victoria prepared for service in church-planting in Rio de Janeiro, Brazil, they went to the Brazilian Pentecostal Church about fifteen miles from their home. On their recent visit home, Tom thrilled that church by preaching in Portuguese about the work going on in Rio while they shared with him about their ministry in reaching out to the Brazilian community (more than 5,000) outside of Boston.

A couple preparing for service in Latin America attends a Hispanic church. A team getting ready for service in Haiti serves at a Haitian church in the city. A single man on his way to serve in Taiwan becomes a member of the Chinese Evangelical Church in town. The presence of internationals helps train cross-cultural workers for the culture, language, and traditions of the countries to which they go. This reciprocal ministry uniquely reflects the Lausanne Committee for World Evangelization theme: "The whole church takes the whole Gospel to the whole world."

The Best Story Yet

In his *Enabler* newsletter, Nate Mirza recounted the following story—perhaps the most amazing contemporary account of God working through a Christian committed to befriending an international who was all alone:

> In 1986, an Englishman, Graham Lacey, and some friends were in New York. They asked themselves who would be the loneliest man in New York City. Concluding it was the Libyan ambassador, they invited him to Thanksgiving dinner. He surprised them by showing up and said, "If people knew who I am, they would spit in my face. Your country has just bombed mine. Your people don't like Colonel Moammar Gadhafi, my leader."
>
> After several weeks of interaction with him, Lacey received an invitation from Gadhafi to visit Libya in August 1987. During an audience with the leader in his Bedouin tent, Lacey was accused of believing a Zionist lie. He answered, "Sir, I know Jesus Christ personally. I've

experienced Him in my life."

After more than an hour's discussion, Lacey asked to pray with Gadhafi. Following discussion with his advisers, the Colonel looked him straight in the face and said, "Sir, you may pray."

"I prayed in the name of our Lord and Savior," Lacey said, "for (Gadhafi's) salvation, for his wife's and his family's, and for revival, for an unprecedented outpouring of the Holy Spirit's power in Libya."

Gadhafi embraced him and after more discussion with his advisers in Arabic, Lacey was told, "The distinguished leader would like you to pray again." As Lacey hesitated, Gadhafi told him, "Nobody has ever told me before about Jesus. Nobody but a Muslim has ever prayed with me. I would like you to get down on your knees and pray again. This time Libyan television will televise it."[7]

Chapter Five

GOING GLOBAL

*To live life to the fullest,
you have to
experience the world.*
Henry Stanley

The bumper sticker caught my eye: THINK GLOBALLY, ACT LOCALLY. The theme rings true for any who aspire to grow as world-class Christians. God calls us to think (and pray and give and understand and live) with a global perspective and to act to affect lives right around us for the advancement of His kingdom.

But our local involvement also thrusts us outward. We desire to grow in our understanding of God's world, so we go beyond our normal comfort zones into involvement with other people from other cultures and (if possible) in other parts of the world.

Going global introduces us to risks. It is risky to try to relate to someone from a culture different from our own. It is risky to travel overseas to places where standards of hygiene are different than we might be accustomed to. It is a challenge to try to communicate with someone who does not speak our language.

Risk goes hand in hand with adventure. As we step out and take risks, we trust God in new ways which deepen our faith and make our Christian commitment come to life. Paul Tournier, the great Swiss psychologist, writes:

> Throughout the history of the church, it has been this reversal in attitude [the desire for security and a risk-free environment] that has raised up martyrs and the heroes of the faith, has given them their indomitable strength, their complete independence as regards men and events, even at the times of greatest failure. . . . What matters is to listen to [God], to let ourselves be guided, to face up to the adventure to which He calls us, with all its risks. Life is an adventure directed by God.[1]

Low-Risk Starters

Paratroopers do not start by jumping out of a plane; they start by jumping off platforms, getting used to the parachutes, and addressing their fears of height from the ground. Going global does not start with getting on a jet for the first time and leaving for the remotest jungles of Papua New Guinea, but it might start with correspondence with a worker from Wycliffe Bible Translators or New Tribes Mission in Papua New Guinea.

We can feel free to start small. Taking the risk of going out to eat international food might be all we can take. Eating "hot salsa sauce" at the Mexican restaurant might be a risk for us, but let's do it! Rationalizing that "Since I am not headed overseas, I need not have an interest in anyplace other than my home culture" misses the opportunity to learn in our ever-shrinking global village.

Larry Anzivino, the chairman of the missions committee at Grace Chapel, encourages these low-risk starters for families and singles desiring to build world-class households:

● Host a missionary and hear about life in a foreign culture. Help children see that people actually live in the countries they see on the map.

● Write to missionaries or foreign friends. (Author's note: of all of the influences that got me thinking about the world, the earliest I can remember was the impact of foreign coins and stamps on letters from international friends. Looking at these introduced me, as a child, to the fascinating reality that our "world" was not the only world.)

● Host an international student or a

friend from another culture for dinner. Help the children know people of different cultures, skin color, and language.

● House an exchange student for a year; this truly internationalizes the family.

● Attend cultural events in ethnic neighborhoods to develop an appreciation for other traditions.

● Eat out together at an international restaurant once a month.

● Keep a stack of prayer cards at the dinner table and pray for one missionary every time there is a family meal.

● Support an international project or a child overseas as a family.

● Take a vacation with a purpose (within the United States) to help at a missions headquarters or to serve by helping in a Vacation Bible School in an ethnic church.

● Make a phone call overseas to bring the work of our international friends into our world.

An article in *Moody Monthly* instructed readers on "How to Be a Foreign Missionary . . . Without Leaving Home."[2] Through prayer, correspondence, and a personal strategy, the author demonstrated how we can serve overseas by being partners with international workers there—even if we never go ourselves. When we start going global with even these small risks, we open a new world of growth for ourselves and our families.

Medium-Range Risks

After we grow accustomed to the international outreach we can have from our home base, we can venture out a little farther. Now the risks and the investments take on greater commitments.

The Stevens family read prophetic words in an article by Tom Sine: "The United States and Western Europe of the nineties will continue to become more ethnically diverse.... Young people raised in the all-white suburbs of America and able to converse in only one language will become the culturally disadvantaged of the nineties. They will be ill-equipped to participate in the increasingly cross-cultural and transnational environment of tomorrow's world."[3]

Not wanting their children or themselves to be "culturally disadvantaged," Mr. and Mrs. Stevens enrolled in a Spanish course in a community college night school and encouraged their children to take Spanish in school. The family went on to commit themselves to serving in a Hispanic neighborhood in the city twice a year, and they try to worship at a Spanish-speaking congregation four times a year to help their language fluency and broaden their understanding of the Christian church.

Language learning is time-consuming, humiliating, and sometimes frustrating, but it is a definite commitment to expand our cultural diversity in the internationalized world in which we live.

For the people at our church (a predominantly white, middle-class, suburban church), medium-range risks include service ventures into the city. John Perkins, leader of the Harambee Christian Center in Los Angeles, exhorts Christians against the "Dangers of a Homogeneous Fellowship"; he encourages everyone to have Christian brothers and sisters from many racial and ethnic backgrounds. He observes that "belonging to a group whose members are like oneself requires no faith. . . . Reconciling bigots is a far greater sign of the supernatural than is speaking in tongues."[4]

One of our young people, Margie Hanson, entered her first heterogeneous fellowship when she went to serve in the inner city. Her experiences were written up in *Campus Life* magazine as an example for other teenagers:

> Margie's job in Newark (New Jersey) was to help in a day-care center with first- and second-graders. "When I first walked into the room and saw all these little black kids, I thought, I'll never be able to tell them apart"—a stereotype she didn't even know she held.
>
> But within a day, she could not only tell them apart, she had fallen in love with them. . . . Margie went to Newark

expecting to give, to help. Instead, she says, she was mostly on the receiving end, and she learned a lot about giving. Margie and the five others on the trip lived with several single mothers in government housing. . . . "They gave up their bedrooms for us. It was very hot that week and they gave us the only fan. They would get up early and make us an incredible breakfast every morning. They'd always wait up for us at night and do other little things, like put a Hershey kiss on our pillows."

Those two weeks in the inner city—two weeks in which she was the minority, the only white face in a sea of black faces—changed Margie. She realized that while she can walk away from the reality of interracial tensions after two weeks in the inner city—because she is white—many people can't. She determined to make a difference where she could.[5]

The experience of going cross-cultural in the city changed Margie's life and worldview. She went to college determined to work in the city, and at this writing, she serves at an orphanage in Calcutta, India.

Going global might not involve international travel. For Carol, it means a weekly trip to a homeless shelter to deliver meals that she and other homemakers have prepared. For Karl and Karen, it means leading a youth group of Cambodian refugees' children. For Ben, it means offering his painting services to inner-city ministries.

One other idea: Consider the people with disabilities. Although they are usually not from a different culture in the usual sense, they do have a subculture of their own that needs to be penetrated with the love of Christ. And yet, the risks we take are real; we will feel awkward at first working with people who are chronically ill, hearing-impaired, blind, or mentally ill. But just as Margie Hanson grew through service in the inner city, we will place ourselves in a new environment where we are required to trust God when we serve those with disabilities.

Medium-range risks take us into the world where people from other cultures and races actually live so that we might, in a small way, identify with them and their worlds. Following the example of Jesus (John 1:14), involvement sends us out to incarnate His love.

Higher and Wider Risks

A travel agency near Harvard University advertises travel with three words: "Please . . . Go Away." In the world of Adoniram Judson, the first white missionary sent from the shores of North America, global travel for the average person was out of the question. It took him three months to sail from the East Coast of the United States to India. Today, however, we can travel from New York City to India in less than two days.

Edie Irish of Flint, Michigan illustrates the world of travel open to us. A member of the Traveler's Century Club (reserved for those who have visited 100 or more foreign countries), this sixty-one-year-old grandmother has now set foot on 293 of the world's 308 nations and island groups. By making travel her priority, she has opened herself to all manner of exploration and risk, recently completing a trip to Libya and planning one to Angola and Chad.[6]

Traveling into other countries and experiencing other cultures is open to us as never before. With appropriate planning and saving, all of us can venture out to have our worldviews expanded by travel. The writers of *Travel and Leisure* observe that "Americans have come to look upon travel as a necessity—even a right—rather than as an extravagance."[7]

Bob expands his view of the missions world by extending his international business trips. His position has him overseas four times per year, and he uses free time and weekends to visit national churches, encourage international workers, and learn about the stresses of cross-cultural adaptation. His growth comes with a risk because it means leaving the secu-

rity of Americanized compounds or conference centers and getting out on the streets of
Hong Kong, Bogota, or Nairobi, but by making advance contact with missionaries or local
believers, he is escorted by people who know
the language and culture.

Hank is a single man who spends his leisure time on cross-cultural trips. He leads
missions service teams or simply travels with
some of the "adventure travel" groups in an
effort to grow in his world vision. These vaca-
tions-with-a-purpose have resulted in Hank's
service on the missions committee and increased financial commitments to international projects.

Short-term mission efforts that were once
reserved for collegians are now available to
adults of all ages. They give us the chance to
visit the missionaries we support, see the
work of the Gospel in another country, meet
Christian sisters and brothers overseas, and
grow in our understanding of the world. Consider some examples:

● My sixty-seven-year-old mother recently
returned from her first-ever mission trip/
vacation to a Third World country. She was
willing to take the risk because a seventy-
year-old friend challenged her to join in the
expedition!

● Willow Creek Community Church, listed
by *Christianity Today* as the largest church in
America, prioritizes short-term missions trips

because "we feel that one way to educate our people to God's worldwide program is through hands-on involvement. So short-term ministries into Mexico, even to the Inner City of Chicago and elsewhere, form a primary emphasis in our ministry."[8]

● Organizations like Wycliffe Associates[9] or Hard Hats for Christ involve construction personnel in voluntary overseas service, especially at times of the year when business is slow back in the United States.

● Chris Eaton, director of Bridge Builders,[10] regularly challenges single adults to use discretionary time and income to serve in overseas opportunities.

Short-term service opportunities should not be some sort of affluent voyeurism, what one person critiqued as "Poor Tours." Instead, they offer involvement: "Get dusty. Stay for two nights with a Mexican family. Learn what the tourists never learn."[11] The higher risks of short-term mission travel are worth it because they offer growth and service opportunities that allow us to live alongside of brothers and sisters from every tribe and tongue and nation, giving us that "preview of heaven" referred to earlier.

Look for These Results
Going global is not merely an excuse for collecting experiences or accumulating new stamps in our passports. Our reason for cross-

cultural involvement is growth as world-class Christians. We go out so that we can grow as people whose lifestyles and obedience are increasingly compatible, in cooperation, and in accord with what God wants to do in our world through us.

When we start taking these low, medium, and high risks, we can look for *significant personal growth.* His travels across Africa in search of Dr. David Livingstone caused Henry Stanley to write, "To live life to the fullest, you have to experience the world." His experiences in other cultures widened his understanding of life itself. Even secular college organizations realize that personal growth comes from selfless service; a new program designed to use students' energy serving (and keeping them away from the raucous parties of Spring Break) advertises itself, "Instead of Beer, Volunteer."

On the Christian front, Chris Eaton writes, "Everybody says they go to serve and give, and every year they come back saying, 'I couldn't give enough compared to what the people gave me. What I learned far outweighs what I taught.' "[12] A student returned from a summer of cross-cultural service and wrote, "God taught me I was never alone. He was with me always. And every time that I was weak, He was strong. Every single time! He would always seem to turn my particular weakness into His strength, and that was amazing to see."[13]

On personal trips overseas or into other cultural settings in our own country, I have noticed that I pray more, consciously trust God more, and grow more. The heightened awareness of being out of control of my own life and trusting it to God makes my faith come to life in a new way.

When we go global, we can also look for *an enlarged perspective*. A recent injury on the basketball court led to surgery and three months in a cast. Although I struggled with the normal self-pity that accompanies any such inconvenience, I realized how overseas travel had changed my perspective. I could not complain. I had clean hospitals to go to and expert surgeons to consult with. A similar injury in a poorer, more remote part of our world might have left me crippled for life.

We do not go overseas or into new cultures to exert some sort of expertise we found through reading travel books. We go as servants and as learners. We go, asking God to change our perspectives, opening ourselves to the changes He wants to make in us based on what we see and experience. In training our summer short-term mission teams, we tell them that one of the purposes of our service is to help us understand that United States culture is not the standard by which all others are measured. We want them to be open to a change in perspective.

Dale Hanson Bourke, former editor of *Today's Christian Woman,* writes of her change in perspective that came as a result of a trip into another culture:

> I had just returned from a trip to Latin America, and the shock of reentry into American society was fresh. Everywhere I turned, I was amazed by our abundance of *things.* In the grocery superstore, for example, I stared at the produce department for several minutes, suppressing my desire to gather up the shiny red apples . . . and send them to the children I had seen begging on the streets of Guatemala City just a few days before. . . .
>
> I looked at the rack of reduced items and realized that the people I had seen living on the city dump would find the overripe fruit and dented cans to be unimaginable treasures.[14]

She goes on to describe her perspectives on contrasts. With the poor in the barrios of Latin America, she had seen a love of children and a wealth of sharing. With the rich in the United States superstore, she saw children abused and people living with dulled moral sensitivities. "I had seen wealth in spirit amidst poverty, and now I saw poverty disguised by wealth."[15]

When we go global, we can look for an *in-*

crease in our witness. Those who spend their vacation time on medical caravans with the Christian Medical Society in Honduras get to share with their peers what they did. This sharing usually leads to an explanation of why they did it.

Friends who spend one weekend per month serving in the inner city often have great opportunities to share their faith with coworkers at Monday's coffee break when the discussion centers on "What did you do this weekend?" The outward expression of Christian faith through cross-cultural serving gives credibility to our commitment, and people stand up and notice.

Christie and I have noticed that overseas service has given us the opportunity to share the Gospel with friends here at home who knew we were "religious" but never heard the Gospel. After our trips to places like Colombia or Nepal or Mozambique, they asked, "Why would you want to go there?" Our answers give us the chance to explain about what it means to be given over to the lordship of Jesus Christ.

Indiana Joneses for Jesus

The young boys in the Christian Service Brigade braced themselves for another boring speaker. It was "missions night," and some feared the worst. To their surprise, the speaker started, "How would you like to be an Indiana Jones for Jesus?"

The boys started to perk up, thinking, "Let's hear more about this."

"What is it that attracts us to the exploits of Indiana Jones?" he asked.

Boys started to raise their hands and fire out ideas:

"He lives a life of adventure."

"He goes to exotic places."

"He eats weird things."

"He hangs around with interesting people."

"He confronts evil powers."

"He seeks after and finds treasures."

"He lives on the edge of danger."

Then the speaker, a missions executive, described how the worldwide call of God needs young people who are willing to be Indiana Joneses for Jesus. He explained with stories about the need for men and women who would go out and take risks—even the risk of dying—to spread the Gospel. These adventurers for Jesus might go to places our world thinks are exotic—like Bombay, Kathmandu, Santiago, or Moscow—to tell people there about the Lord. Strange foods, fascinating people, exposure to the powers of Satan, and guaranteed danger lay ahead for those who followed God's call into other cultures. But, like Indiana Jones, they would persevere because they were after the greatest treasure of all: the treasure of seeing others come to know Jesus Christ.

The boys generally agreed that the missions speaker "wasn't as boring as we'd expected," and they went home dreaming of the risks that Jesus might call them to take.

If, as Tournier says, "life is an adventure directed by God," we face the challenge of being adventurers for Jesus. Will you step out and go global (even if it is only short-term) in an effort to understand and be more aware of our world? Taking such a risk will change your life.

Chapter Six

YOU CAN BE A WORLD-CLASS CHRISTIAN!

No reserve. No retreat.
No regrets.
William Borden

My wife and I have tried to apply the principle of living more simply when we purchase a car. We never purchase a brand-new model, and we have preferred a "seasoned," older model. In light of the costs of the car, the excise tax, and the insurance rates in our state, older cars have saved us considerable amounts of money.

One car we purchased, a pumpkin-orange Volvo, had over 100,000 miles on it. Nevertheless, it lasted for quite a while (we retired it with 172,000 miles!). Its last winter, however, the mechanical problems intensified. The car would not start so we called the tow truck. After a few days in the shop, the mechanic told us, "I can get this baby started, but you'll never keep it going." We laid the car to rest in the junkyard.

When considering the incredible task of being world-class Christians, we feel like that old Volvo. "I can get my vision started. I can get excited about a few statistics, a good book, or an exciting speaker, but I'll never be able to keep my vision going. I'm already worn out, so sustaining world-class Christian growth is beyond me."

We might get started, but can we keep going? All of us get wide-eyed at the prospect of thinking of global issues, international outreach, or praying for world missions. We can barely make it through the winter or manage our household budget; how can we start caring about 1 billion people in China or the hungry in Latin America?

While none of us can fathom the vastness or the scope of world missions, we can start small and build our vision as part of our ongoing discipleship. In addition to increasing our appreciation for the awesomeness of the God we serve, a growing world vision will help us keep our personal problems in proper perspective.

Keeping Going Won't Be Easy

"Why do we get such great attendance at our Christmas pageants, but such dismal attendance at missions events?" The question stung. A concerned, internationally aware

Christian was simply observing the obvious. I gave a few trite answers in immediate response, but his question got me thinking.

Was it because our presentations were shabby? Perhaps, but we had been making concerted efforts to overcome this.

Was it because our speakers were boring? Maybe, but we had hosted some of the top missions speakers in the country, and the turnout at our meetings was still poor.

I finally realized that the focus of the two events was different. The Christmas pageant was musical, festive, and culturally acceptable. Although the Gospel message was present, it came in the form of a celebration related to a popular holiday.

In contrast, the essence of international, cross-cultural ministry is sacrifice. The Gospel is still present, but in the form of cross-bearing unselfishness and giving. The Christmas pageant could satisfy those that came to receive; world-focus meetings were for those ready to give.

The experience of evaluation forced me to realize that the challenge of being a world-class Christian is truly counter-cultural. Asking for unselfishness, sacrifice, and Christlike service is foreign to a culture where our first question is often, "What's in this for me?"

Events that focus on international needs and cross-cultural service opportunities may never get the same type of attendance as concerts, Christmas pageants, or Easter services, but this may be because the world-class Christian challenge has not been understood.

Keeping the Vision Going

Managerial experts frequently use the saying, "Failing to plan is planning to fail." The saying holds true for our personal growth as world-class Christians. If we do not plan for expanding our vision through reading, prayer, experiences in serving, or simpler living, it probably will not happen.

To develop a growth plan, keep in mind this definition of what it means to be a world-class Christian: *A world-class Christian is one whose lifestyle and obedience are compatible, in cooperation, and in accord with what God is doing and wants to do in our world.*

Keeping our vision going and growing means reading slowly over that definition and asking, "Where are my strengths? Where are my weak spots? Where do I need to start growing?"

Everyone of us needs to grow in some aspect of that definition. Perhaps the best idea is to look over the following five areas and ask, "What goal could I set over the next year to assist my growth in these areas?"

Information. After one Sunday School class, a young man told me that he was going to commit himself that day to reading the international section of the newspaper. He said, "I usually read only the sports section, but I am growing to understand that God may want to use that newspaper as my guide for prayer today."

A world-class vision cannot grow without fueling the vision with information. Subscribing to *World Christian* magazine,[1] getting on a missionary's mailing list, or (if we are really zealous) getting the round-the-world "Pulse" report published by the Evangelical Missions Information Service[2] will help us get a better idea of some of the challenges facing the church worldwide.

Information growth might include learning geography (i.e., finding out the location of Guyana, Guinea-Bissau, Equatorial Guinea, or Papua New Guinea) or reading a biography of some great missionary.

Here are some sample goals that could be set by an individual or a study group for the next month, six months, or year. Informational growth is not limited to these suggestions; these are simply samples, but feel free to add your own:

● Buy an up-to-date map of the world or an atlas.

● Learn the countries of the world (or perhaps the countries of one specific continent).

● Do a study through the entire Bible to document God's commission to go into the whole world with the Gospel.

● Read *From Jerusalem to Irian Jaya* by Ruth Tucker (the documentation of Christian history through the collection of missionary biographies).

● Read one book on missions theology or one specific missionary biography.

● Attend an informational conference or seminar either on missions or on some issue in our world today.

● Do a personal research study on one country, culture, or issue of global concern (such as global warming, communism, or the rich/poor gap).

● Buy a global-learning game to help your family or friends grow in geographic knowledge.

● Subscribe to *National Geographic* or some other source of international information.

● View a movie or video which will encourage your learning about some other part of the world.

The best fuel for world-class growth is information.

Intercession. Responding in prayer challenges our busy schedules because it takes time. It also challenges our faith because we may wrestle with our doubts about prayer's viability.

To build our vision in this area, it is important to look to the psalmist and realize that praising God for being the Lord of the whole earth is our starting point (Pss. 19:1; 46:10; 66:7; 67:4, 7). Worship reminds us of the Lord of the harvest, and all other needs that we bring before Him take on perspective under Him.

Many of the world needs are so vast that we feel compelled to respond in prayer, committing needs to God when we can make no other response. Patrick Johnstone's *Operation World* (Zondervan) can help us learn about and pray for the world, or we may want to focus on the needs of one specific missionary. I start almost every meeting by thanking God for the freedom that we have to meet together as Christians; it's one small effort I can make to sensitize myself and others to those Christians who suffer for their faith in other parts of our world.

"What if I am struggling to pray faithfully for my family and friends? How can I add the world?"

We don't need to pray for the whole world, but we can expand our prayer horizons by adding one or two missions-related prayers to our daily intercession. We can pray with bifocal vision and grow.

Here are some suggested goals:

● Use *Operation World* each week to start a Sunday School class or a weekly

Bible study. Read the entry of the day and ask one or two people to pray about it.

● Ask for a missionary's prayer letter.

● Do a study of biblical prayers, paying special attention to what they teach about the character, mercy, and outreach of God.

● Read Wesley Duewels *Touch the World Through Prayer* (Zondervan).

● Contact Overseas Missionary Fellowship for information on the regional prayer conferences they sponsor throughout the country. Ask also for their brochure by Bill Wilson, "7 Ways to Pray for Your Missionary."

● Watch the news regularly (or read a weekly newsmagazine) and practice "arrow" prayers.

● Read the biographies of either Hudson Taylor or George Müller to stimulate conviction about prayer.

● Start praying for one country or "people group" as you learn about it.

Paul exhorted the Thessalonians to "pray without ceasing" (1 Thes. 5:17, NASB). With a world before us, we will have plenty to "pray without ceasing" about.

Integration. Jeff and Judy are newlyweds; they are committed to grow in their world-class vision. As a result, they have determined that integration of that vision with daily life means trying to avoid the trap of accumulating things. "When you are first married," they observe, "you think to yourself, 'Wow, our apartment is so empty; we need this and we need that.' We have watched our married friends, and it takes no time at all to get bogged down with 'stuff.' As a result, we try to keep away from unnecessary purchases. God may send us to some developing country to serve, and we figure that it is good experience for us to get accustomed to living with less."

Because they have become aware of the lifestyles of those outside their own country, Jeff and Judy have chosen to live more simply that others may simply live.

If we do not incorporate our world missions learning into our daily lives, it will become mundane or irrelevant. We start integrating a world-class vision into our lives by listening to international reports on the news, reading about places we have never heard of in *National Geographic*, or putting a world map over our desks. (My wife and I have tried to integrate a reminder of the great world into which we are called by surrounding ourselves with world maps—place mats, a desk blotter, a pencil sharpener, a clock, a paperweight, and even a beach ball all set the world before us regularly!)

On the next page are some suggested goals

to keep the vision of an integrated lifestyle growing:

- Do a Bible study on riches, stewardship, or management of resources.
- Read Tom Sine's *Mustard Seed Conspiracy, Why Settle for More and Miss the Best?* or *Wild Hope* (all published by Word).
- See if you can increase your financial giving 1/2 to 1 percent this month.
- Find an overseas project to which your Bible study or Sunday School class can give an annual gift.
- Label the coat hangers in your closet. The first time you wear the clothes, take the label off that hanger. After one year (or three to six months, whatever you determine), give away any of the clothes on hangers which still have labels. If we can go one year without wearing it, we can find someone who can use it more.
- Read Ronald Sider's *Rich Christians in an Age of Hunger* (InterVarsity Press).
- Next time you shop for clothes, buy something to be donated for use at a shelter for homeless people (Shelters have a crying need for underwear!).
- Give something away!
- Join with friends once per month or week to skip a meal and donate the costs to a relief agency.
- Challenge yourself to go for a week or

month without saying, "I'm hungry," "I feel starved," or "I need. . . ."

● Take a half day sometime over the next year to do a personal evaluation, asking questions like, "Where could I simplify my life?" "Am I being motivated by kingdom-of-God or materialistic values?" or "How can I develop greater thankfulness for all I have?"

Involvement. "Give me something to do." The speaker, a young activist from our college group, desperately wanted to put what he had learned into practice. He wanted to be a doer of the Word, not merely a hearer (James 1:22).

As our vision for God's world grows, we need to find ways to respond practically. Writing letters to encourage missionaries, setting aside time each year to get involved in a service project, or adopting an orphan from another country all serve to expand our sense of participation in God's diverse world.

Here are some practical goals to consider:

● Get some training on how to share the Gospel with friends and coworkers.

● Investigate the opportunities to reach out to immigrants or international students in the local community (or at nearby colleges).

● Take your Sunday School class or Bible study group on a field trip into a new culture—this could mean an international meal together, a worship service with a church from a different ethnic background, or a partnership in serving some need in the community.

● Look into the possibility of an overseas short-term experience, perhaps serving with one of your church's supported mission families.

● Participate in a project at an inner-city ministry.

● Learn a few greetings in another language, preferably one spoken by people who live nearby.

● Start praying for and targeting ways to reach out to subgroups in the community that may usually be overlooked (the police, night shift workers, the medical community, etc.).

● Write a letter every month simply to encourage a missionary serving in another culture.

● Host a missionary in your home and invite friends to come meet him or her.

● Organize an international student dinner at your church over one of the holidays (when they may be in the dormitories and most lonely).

Don't just stand there; do something!

Investigation. At some point in time, as our vision grows, we will all have to wrestle with the questions: "What about me?" "Where do I fit?" "Where do I need to grow toward fulfilling God's design for me in this great world?" "Should I consider cross-cultural ministry?"

Opening ourselves to the lordship of Christ is basic to Christian growth. Perhaps He will call us into missions work, but He may direct us to stay right where we are. We will never know without opening ourselves totally to Him.

Some possible goals regarding investigation might be to:

- Read a book on discerning the will of God like *A Slow and Certain Light* by Elisabeth Elliot (Abingdon) or *Decision-Making and the Will of God* by Garry Friesen (Multnomah).
- Experiment with God's call by getting involved in a ministry and discover if you have the gifts and abilities to match the requirements.
- Look for opportunities to be a world-minded catalyst in your church, perhaps by joining (or starting) the international missions committee or by helping to present the global challenge to others.
- Evaluate your retirement plans now; how could you use those golden years in some sort of cross-cultural service?
- Look into the needs for "tentmakers" to limited access countries. Could your profession help gain entry to a country

where missionaries are not allowed?
● Ask others to help you discover your gifts and abilities.
● Mobilize others for world concerns by giving them manageable tasks for learning or growth.
● Commit your children or grandchildren to the Lord, even if that means their involvement in some international setting.

All of us have some part to play in God's worldwide plan, but it may take some serious investigation to discover exactly where He may want us in the days ahead.

Just Do It!

Growing as world-class Christians requires the discipline of exercise. In the same way that we combat the procrastination and excuses that keep us from jogging, biking, or swimming, we will need diligence to continue to grow with a world vision. The folks at Nike athletic shoes give us the exhortation we need; we know what needs to be done—JUST DO IT!

When I am prone to quit the task of trying to make world-class growth a priority in my own life, I remember people. I am motivated by the changes in people as they have opened their eyes to God's world and their hearts to God's service.

I remember . . .

Bryan and Janet, who have opened themselves to full-time ministry in a "second career" phase of their lives because they have been surrounded by world-class Christian friends;

Marion, who chose to go to Haiti to serve meals rather than enjoy the rocking chair of retirement;

David, who is using his international business travel to encourage missionaries and national workers in the countries he visits;

Debbie and Norm, who got started learning about India by inviting an Indian family over to their home for their first taste of pizza;

Nathan, who, at age five, does not have a broad world vision, but he is learning to say "Africa" with excitement;

Bob, who has worked out his own international vision by leading over fifteen service teams and by serving behind the scenes at our international student functions.

All of these people have enlarged their vision for the world by investigating how God wanted to use them to have a global impact on their local church. These—and dozens of others changed by a greater view of God and His world—encourage me to continue toward the goal of being a world-class Christian.

In the 1800s, A.T. Pierson saw the Christian opportunity in his world, "a combination of grand opportunity and great responsibility; chance of glorious success or awful failure."

Gordon Aeschliman observes that even greater opportunities face us as we approach the year 2000:

> Never before has the shadow of the church been cast so far into distant places. Every tribe created by the hand of God now lives within the reach of Christians, be it through commerce, education, medicine, government, or neighborhood guilds.
>
> Our hour is unprecedented, our jungle is uncharted, our opportunities are unmatched. There is only one village left in our day, and it is called Planet Earth. To be a member of God's international family as humanity steps into the twenty-first century is perhaps the closest we'll get to heaven in the flesh.[3]

LET'S DO IT!

Looking outward—developing a bigger view of the world—is an essential part of our continued world-class growth as followers of Christ. This list of books, magazines, and organizations is designed to help us maintain an outward orientation in our faith.

Books, Magazines, and Prayer Guides

Bakke, Ray. *The Urban Christian*. Downers Grove, Ill.: InterVarsity Press, 1987.

Banks, William L. *In Search of the Great Commission*. Chicago: Moody Press, 1991.

Borthwick, Paul. *A Mind for Missions*. Colorado Springs: NavPress, 1987.

Christenson, Evelyn. *What Happens When Women Pray*. Wheaton, Ill.: Victor Books, 1976.

Coleman, Robert. *Great Commission Lifestyle*. Grand Rapids: Fleming H. Revell, 1992.

Duewel, Wesley L. *Touch the World through Prayer*. Grand Rapids: Zondervan, 1986.

Elliot, Elisabeth. *Shadow of the Almighty: The Life and Testament of Jim Elliot*. San Francisco: Harper and Row, 1979.

Frontier Fellowship Prayer Guide. Published monthly by the U.S. Center for World Mission, 1605 East Elizabeth Street, Pasadena, CA 91104.

Johnstone, Patrick. *Operation World*. Grand Rapids: Zondervan, 1993.

McClung, Floyd. *Living on the Devil's Doorstep*. Waco, Texas: Word, 1988.

National Geographic. Washington, D.C. 20036.

Operation Mobilization Prayer Cards. OM Lit., P.O. Box 28, Waynesboro, GA 30830.

Seiple, Robert A. *One Life at a Time.* Waco, Texas: Word, 1990.

Short-Term Mission Handbook. Berry Publishing Services, 701 Main Street, Evanston, Ill. 60202.

Sine, Tom, *Why Settle for More and Miss the Best?* Waco, Texas: Word, 1987.

Stepping Out: A Guide to Short-term Missions. Monrovia, Calif.: Short-Term Advocates, 1987.

Tucker, Ruth. *From Jerusalem to Irian Jaya.* Grand Rapids: Zondervan, 1983.

Organizations

Advancing Churches in Missions Commitment, P.O. Box ACMC, Wheaton, IL 60189.

Concerts of Prayer, International, Pentagon Towers, P.O. Box 36008, Minneapolis, MN 55435.

Evangelical Missions Information Service, P.O. Box 794, Wheaton, IL 60189.

Food for the Hungry, 7729 East Greenway Rd., Scottsdale, AZ 85260.

InterVaristy Christian Fellowship, Missions Department, P.O. Box 7895, Madison, WI 53707-7895.

Operation Mobilization, P.O. Box 444, Tyrone, GA 30290.

Overseas Missionary Fellowship, 10 West Dry Creek Circle, Littleton, CO 80120.

U.S. Center for World Mission, 1605 East Elizabeth Street, Pasadena, CA 91104.

World Relief Commission, P.O. Box WRC, Wheaton, IL 60189.

World Vision, 919 West Huntington Drive, Monrovia, CA 91016.

Notes

Chapter One

1. Howard Foltz, Missions Link, vol. 1, no. 7 August 1989, 1.
2. Tom Sine, "Will the Real Cultural Christian Please Stand Up?" *World Vision,* October/November, 1989, 21.
3. "Lord of the Universe, Hope of the World" was the theme of InterVarsity's Urbana 90 Convention.
4. The term "Great Commission" refers to the final mandate of Jesus (recorded in various forms in Matt. 28:18-20; Mark 16:15; Luke 24:47; John 20:21; and Acts 1:8); a generally accepted definition summarizes the mandate as "making disciples of all nations." When this Great Commission is accomplished, most scholars believe it will prepare us for the second coming of Jesus (Matt. 24:14).

Chapter Two

1. Brian F. O'Connell, "Understanding Your World," *Discipleship Journal,* Issue 41, 1987, 18.
2. Louis Wigdor, "Taking Global Education Seriously," *The Common Wealth,* Fall 1989, 1–2.
3. Ibid., 2.
4. *Church Around the World* is published monthly by Tyndale House Publishers, P.O. Box 220, Wheaton, IL 60189.
5. Evangelical Missions Information Service, P.O. Box 794, Wheaton, IL 60189.
6. Anagrams by Beatrice Bachrach Perri. Answers: (1) Lisbon; (2) Madrid; (3) Helsinki; (4) Paris; (5) Tirana; (6) Prague; (7) Belgrade; (8) Warsaw; (9) Bucharest; (10) Copenhagen; (11) Athens; (12) London.
7. Morris Watkins, *Seven Worlds to Win* (Fullerton, Calif.: R.C. Law, 1987), 9–183.
8. Floyd McClung and Kalafi Moala, *Nine Worlds to Win* (Kailua-Kona, Hawaii: Youth With a Mission, 1988), 51–92.

Chapter Three

1. David Howard, *The Great Commission for Today* (Downers Grove, Ill.: InterVarsity Press, 1976), 98–102.
2. Some of these suggestions appeared in my article "Around the World on Your Knees," *Discipleship Journal,* Issue 48, 1988, 10.
3. From the brochure "How to Pray for Your Missionaries," published by Greater Europe Mission, Box 668, Wheaton, IL 60189.
4. "Prayer Tips: Praying for the Unreached," *Co-Laborer* news

letter (The Caleb Project, P.O. Box 40455, Pasadena, CA 91114), Fall 1989.

5. Portions of this chapter appeared in my article "Sharpen Your Global Prayers," *World Vision*, August/September 1989, 10–11.

Chapter Four

1. Jerry L. Appleby, *Missions Have Come to America* (Kansas City: Beacon Hill Press, 1986), 8–9.

2. Lawson Lau, *The World at Your Doorstep* (Downers Grove, Ill.: InterVarsity Press), 12–13.

3. Kathy Lay, "International Outreach," *Today's Christian Woman*, September 1989, 85.

4. Gordon Loux, "Reach the World from Your Living Room," *World Vision*, Feb.–March, 1990, 11.

5. Adapted from a list by Joy Cordell, "How to Launch a Foreign Friendship," *World Vision*, Feb.–March, 1990, 11.

6. Mark Rentz, "Diplomats in Our Backyard," *Newsweek*, 16 February 1987, 10.

7. Nate Mirza quoted this from *The Baptist Standard*, 28 June 1989.

Chapter Five

1. Paul Tournier, *The Adventure of Living* (New York: Harper and Row, Publishers 1963), 153.

2. Angee Walsh, "How to Be a Foreign Missionary . . . Without Leaving Home," *Moody Monthly*, Dec. 1988, 29–33.

3. Tom Sine, "Shifting into the Future Tense," *Christianity Today*, 17 November 1989, 21.

4. John Perkins, "The Danger of a Homogeneous Fellowship," *World Christian*, May 1990, 18.

5. Diane Eble, "Making a Difference," *Campus Life*, May 1988, 42.

6. "Globe-Hopping Mama," *First*, December 1989, 5.

7. Coleman Lollar, "It's the 1990s: Where Are We Going?" *Travel & Leisure*, January 1990, 135.

8. Jerry Butler, "International Ministries," *Willow Creek*, Nov./Dec. 1989, 27.

9. Wycliffe Associates, P.O. Box 2000, Orange, CA 92669.

10. Bridge Builders, c/o Chris Eaton, 9925 Seventh Way, North, #102, St. Petersburg, FL 33702.

11. "Where in the World!" *Paraclete* (U.S. Center for World Mission newsletter) issue 1, 11.

12. Chris Eaton, "Short-Term Missions for Single Adults: Why and How," *Single Adult Ministries Journal* (February 1988): 3.

13. Quoted in Alice Poyner, *From the Campus to the World*

(Downers Grove, Ill.: InterVarsity Press, 1983), 151.

14. Dale Hanson Bourke, "Better off in Guatemala," *Today's Christian Woman*, Jan./Feb. 1990, 72.
15. Ibid.

Chapter Six
1. *World Christian*, P.O. Box 40010, Pasadena, CA 91104.
2. Evangelical Missions Information Service, P.O. Box 794, Wheaton, IL 60189.
3. Gordon Aeschliman, "Dancing on the Shrinking Globe," *World Christian*, May 1990, 9.